Contents

Equipment and materials

This book describes activities which use the following:

Adhesives (PVA, UHU and Bostik)
Beads
Brass paper fasteners
Brushes (for glue and paint)
Calico (a type of cotton cloth, usually white – an old sheet would do)
Card (ivory board is ideal)
Cardboard boxes
Cellophane (see page 44)
Clay or plasticine
Cloth (scraps)
Coat-hanger
Cold water dyes
Cooking oil
Cork (from a bottle)
Dowel rods
Drawing pins
Face paints
Feathers
Felt (scraps)
Felt pens (water-soluble)
Garden rods or sticks
Gloves (old)
Hole punch
Indian inks
Jam jars (old, for water, and for mixing PVA glue)
Kitchen paper
Knife (blunt)
Lamps (see page 44)

Masking tape
Needles
Newspaper
Paint (poster or tempera paint is suitable for most surfaces; use acrylic paint for plastic)
Paper (white and coloured)
Paper bags
Paper clips
Paper plates
Pen/Pencil
Pins
Plastic fruit-juice bottles (empty)
Polystyrene balls
Polystyrene ceiling tiles
Ruler
Sandpaper
Saucers (old, for mixing paints)
Scarf (old, silk or cotton)
Scissors
Screwdriver
Sequins
Shoe box
Spoon (old)
Staples
String
Thread
Torch
Trimming knife
Vilene
Wire
Wood
Wooden spoons (old)
Wool

Creative Crafts

Puppets

Lyndie Wright

Consultant: Henry Pluckrose

Photography: Chris Fairclough

W

FRANKLIN WATTS
LONDON•SYDNEY

This edition 2004

Franklin Watts
96 Leonard Street
London EC2A 4XD

Franklin Watts Australia
45-51 Huntley Street,
Alexandria, NSW 2015

Hardback edition published
under the series title Fresh Start.

Editor: Jenny Wood
Design: Edward Kinsey

ISBN 0 7496 5895 9

Printed in Belgium

Many years ago, when I was seven or eight years old, I made my first puppet. Forty years later I am still as fascinated as ever, as ideas and possibilities present themselves to excite me anew. The range in puppetry is so vast. From the simplest wooden-spoon puppet to complicated, thirty-stringed marionettes, from the modern abstract shapes to the traditional figures of a thousand years ago, from one-man shows to companies of a hundred – all this is puppetry.

Basically there are four main types of puppet:

1 *String puppets or marionettes*
These are jointed figures worked by strings tied to the figure and to a control (usually a wooden cross) which the puppeteer holds. A variety of materials can be used for the making of a marionette – leather, plywood, plastic wood or cloth – but string puppets are most often carved out of wood.

2 *Rod puppets*
The head and hands of a rod puppet are fixed to the ends of sticks or rods which the puppeteer holds to operate the figure. The body is of cloth, either sewn or draped. The head and hands can be made from wood, plastic wood, cloth or papier mâché. Rod puppets don't usually have legs.

3 *Glove puppets*
The head of a glove puppet can be made from wood, papier mâché or cloth, and the hands from wood or stuffed cloth. The head and hands are attached to a sack-like cloth body and the figure is worn like a glove on the puppeteer's hand. As with rod puppets, glove puppets usually have no legs.

4 *Shadow puppets*
These are flat figures made of cardboard, plastic or specially prepared animal hide. They are worked from behind a translucent screen, with only the shadow of the figure seen by the audience.

There are various ways of putting a show together. You may like to start with a written script from a book of puppet plays, or adapt a story, fairytale or legend. You may like to write your own play based around the puppet characters you have made.

If you write your own piece or adapt a story, try out your ideas with your puppets before completing the script.

Remember that puppets like to do things, not stand about making speeches! And it is only when the figure moves that it becomes a puppet and not just a toy.

Be careful to move only the puppet which is talking, so that your audience know which character is speaking.

From behind the stage or screen it is very difficult to know what your audience is going to be looking at, so have someone sitting out in front during rehearsal to direct you. Practising movements in front of a mirror can also be very helpful.

1 Here are some of the things you will need when painting the puppets and costumes in this book: Indian inks, cold water dyes, powder or tempera paints, water-soluble felt pens, face paints and brushes.

2 Gather together the following glues, threads and fixing materials for making your puppets: PVA glue, UHU and Bostik; masking tape, string and carpet thread.

3 For your sewing kit you will need: calico, needles, threads, embroidery threads, string, wool, beads, sequins, felt and an old glove or two.

The simplest of all puppets are painted fingers and painted hands.

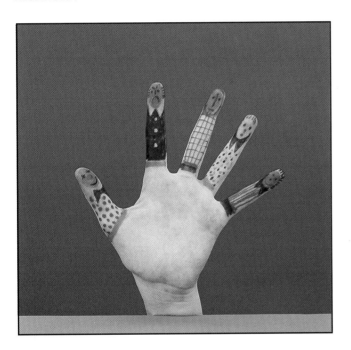

1 You can make an entire puppet company for yourself by drawing the characters on your fingers with water-based, non-toxic felt pens.

2 Face paints are good for hand painting as well as face painting. You can draw either front or side views of your characters' faces. Wash your hands with soap and warm water when your show is over.

Finger puppets

You will need a piece of calico, a pencil, scissors, a needle and thread, water-soluble felt pens, a paintbrush, a jar of water, wool or embroidery thread, and, if required, sequins, beads and scraps of felt.

1 Fold the calico once, to make it double thickness. Place your finger on the folded material and draw round it. Draw a dotted line 1cm away from your first line – this will be your stitching line. Now draw another solid line 1cm away from your dotted line – this will be your cutting line.

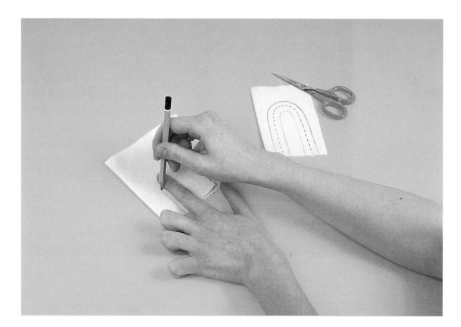

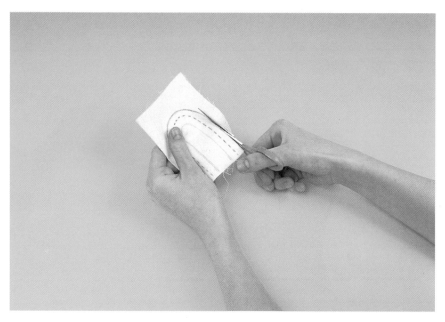

2 Cut along the outer solid line.

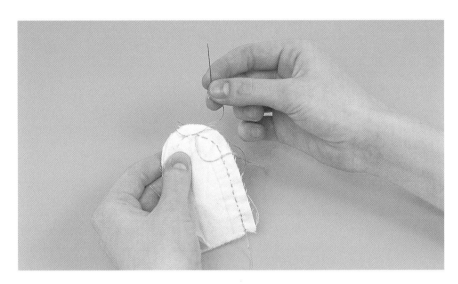

3 Thread the needle with a double thread knotted at the end. Sew along the dotted line using small stitches. Finish off the thread by sewing a few stitches on top of each other.

4 Now turn your stitched finger shape inside out.

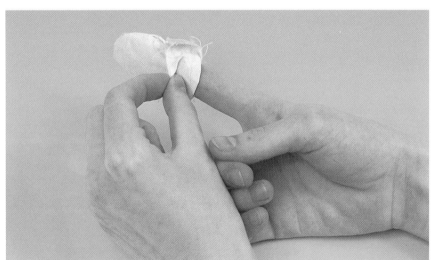

5 Colour your puppet with water-soluble felt pens. To make the colours flow into each other, paint over sections with a wettish brush. Experiment on a scrap of cloth before you paint your puppet to see how wet your brush needs to be. You can draw over the painted areas to strengthen the colours.

6 When your puppet is dry, add embroidery thread or wool for hair. A felt hat may be added and decorated with sequins or small beads.

7 Your puppet or puppets are now ready for putting on a finger-puppet show.

A little finger-puppet stage can be made from an old shoe box. Simply cut away half the bottom of the box and stand the box on end to make a booth. This could look very good painted in stripes like an old Punch and Judy booth.

You will need a piece of calico, a pencil, scissors, a needle and thread, water-soluble felt pens, a paintbrush, a jar of water, and embroidery thread or wool.

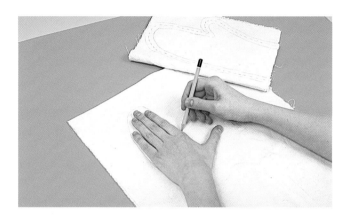

1 Fold the calico once, to make it double thickness. Place your hand on the folded material, fingers together and thumb extended, and draw round it. Draw a dotted line 1cm away from your first line – this will be your stitching line. Now draw another solid line 1cm away from your dotted line – this will be your cutting line.

2 Cut along the outer solid line.

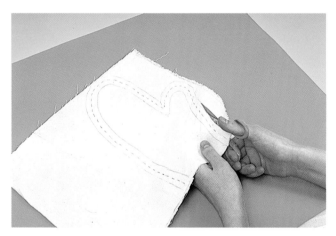

3 Thread the needle with a double thread knotted at the end. Sew along the dotted line using small stitches. Finish off the thread by sewing a few stitches on top of each other.

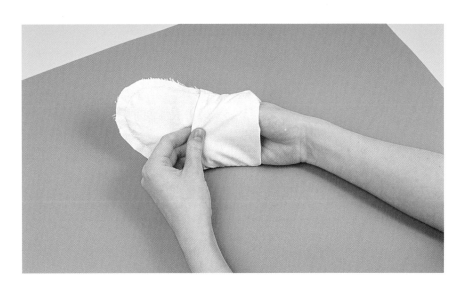

4 Turn your sewn glove inside out.

5 Colour your puppet with water-soluble felt pens, then wash over the colour with a wet brush.

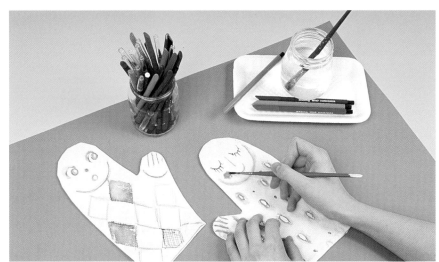

6 Sew wool or embroidery thread on for hair, five or six strands at a time.

7 Your puppet or puppets are now complete and ready to perform.

You will need a wooden spoon, powder or tempera paints, paintbrushes, a jar of water, a saucer, white typing paper, scissors, calico, Indian inks or cold water dyes, masking tape, a feather, and embroidery thread or wool.

1 (Left) Paint a face on to the back of the wooden spoon.

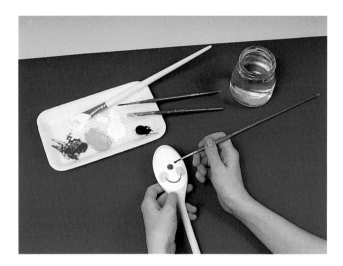

2 (Right, above) Cut out five or six circles of typing paper for the puppet's collar.

3 (Right, below) Pierce a hole in the centre of each circle and thread them on to the spoon handle.

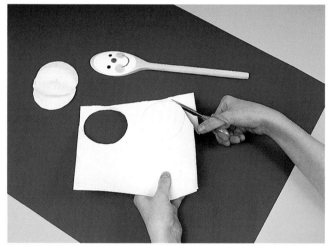

4 (Left) Cut a large circle of white calico, about 45cm in diameter, for your puppet's costume. Paint it with Indian inks or cold water dyes (see page 44). The puppet's neck will be in the centre of the cloth.

5 Cut a small hole in the centre of the cloth circle. Thread the spoon handle through this hole and fasten it to the underside of the material with masking tape.

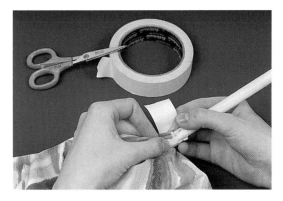

6 Add a feather as hair, or make a thread or wool wig instead. You may even like to make a hat to complete your wooden-spoon puppet.

An interesting puppet could be made from a wooden fork or from a washing-up mop. As you start to think about puppets, you will find that objects at school and in your home give you lots of ideas.

Paper-plate puppets

You will need a white paper plate, Indian inks or powder paints, paintbrushes, a jar of water, a saucer, a flat stick or ruler, masking tape, scissors, a piece of calico painted with Indian inks or dyes, an old glove, pins, a needle and thread, coloured paper, a blunt knife, and glue.

1 Paint a face on to the paper plate using Indian inks or powder paints.

2 Using masking tape, fasten the flat stick or ruler on to the back of the plate.

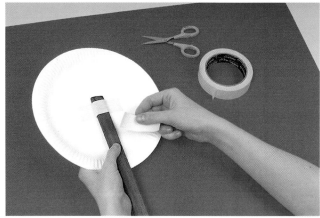

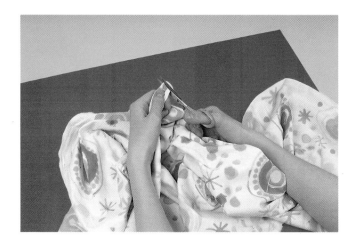

3 Cut a small hole in the centre of the painted calico.

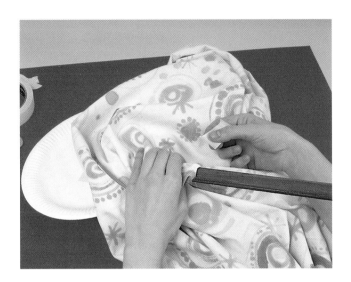

4 Slip the stick through this hole and, at the neck, fasten the underside of the material to the stick with masking tape.

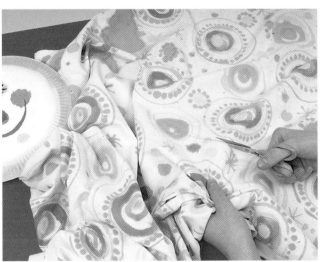

5 About 35cm away from the puppet's neck, make a cut in the cloth the width of your glove.

6 Place the glove into the slit, with the thumb nearest the puppet's head. Pin it, then, on the underside of the material, sew it into position.

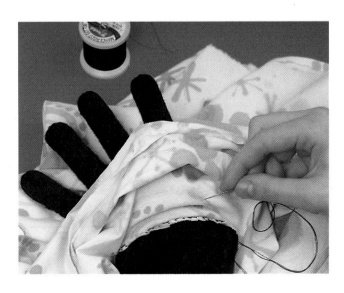

7 To make curly hair for your puppet, cut the coloured paper into strips and stretch them by using the edge of a blunt knife. Hold a paper strip between your thumb and first finger and carefully pull the knife edge along the paper.

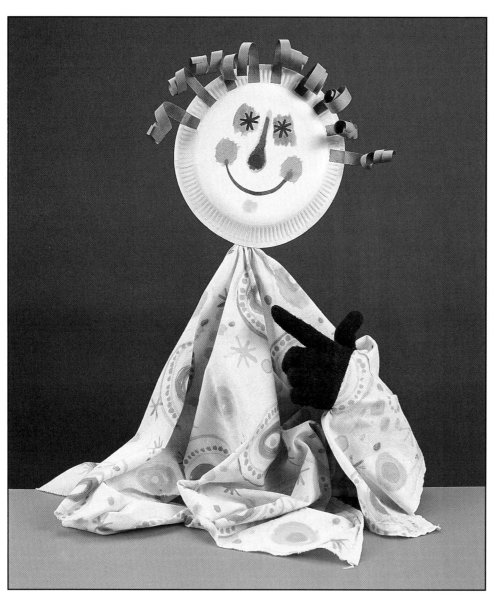

8 Glue the curls on to the paper plate. Your puppet is ready for action!

You will find the glove hand is very useful if you have to handle props. Keep your hand movements simple and clear so that the audience can follow your actions. They must be convinced that the hand belongs to the puppet and not to a person.

You will need newspaper, PVA glue, a glue brush, a dowel rod or stick, drawing pins or staples, two paper bags, masking tape, a jar of water, scissors, kitchen paper, powder or tempera paint, paintbrushes, a saucer, calico, cold water dyes, and wool or embroidery thread.

1 Paint a sheet of newspaper with PVA glue. Be careful to protect the area you are working on with old newspaper, and wipe off any spilt glue before it dries.

2 Roll the newspaper loosely round the end of the dowel rod or stick and fix in place with a staple or drawing pin.

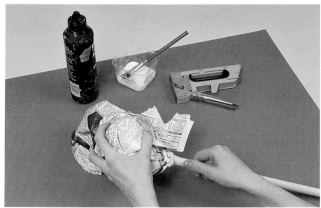

3 Put the lump of newspaper into a double paper bag. Fill the remaining spaces in the bag with more gluey newspaper.

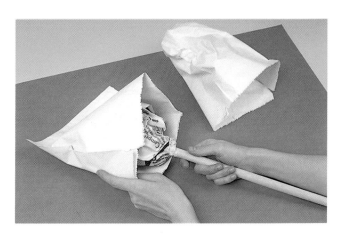

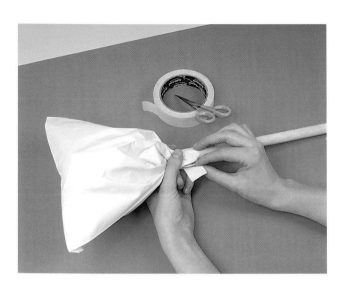

4 Tie up the neck of the bag with masking tape.

5 Flatten the pointed corners. Paint the whole bag with PVA glue (diluted one part glue to one part water) and leave to dry.

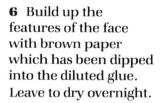

6 Build up the features of the face with brown paper which has been dipped into the diluted glue. Leave to dry overnight.

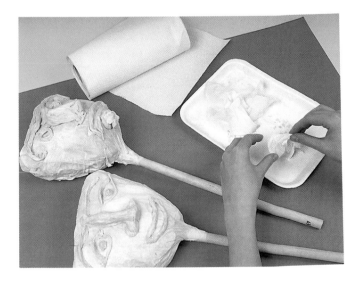

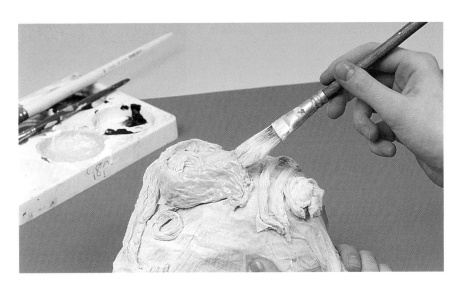

7 You will find that the features have hardened overnight and the head can now be painted with powder or tempera paint.

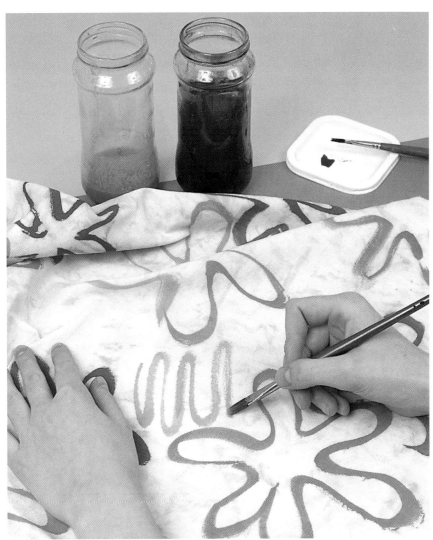

8 Make a costume for your puppet from the calico. Paint it with dye, or use a coloured piece of cloth. Make a neck hole and fasten the cloth to the rod with masking tape. Now decorate your puppet with hair and eyes.

9 Two finished paper-bag puppets.

If you need to handle props, you could use a glove hand as with the paper-plate puppets on pages 16–18.

You will need a plastic fruit-juice bottle, scissors, masking tape, a dowel rod, old newspaper, PVA glue, a jar of water, a glue brush, sandpaper, calico, a pencil, a needle and thread, powder or tempera paint, paintbrushes, a saucer, bits and pieces for decorating your puppet (felt, feathers, beads, wool), fabric for your puppet's costume, Bostik, and Indian inks or cold water dyes.

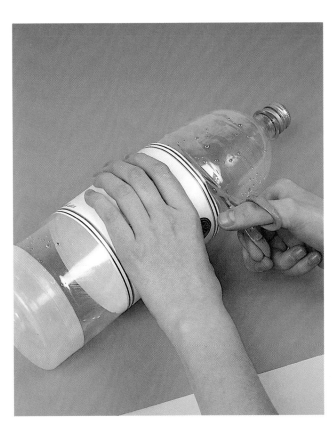

1 Cut the top third off the fruit-juice bottle. This top third will be the neck end of your puppet's head.

2 Cut off the bottom third. (The middle section of the bottle can be thrown away.) Cut or pull off the base of the bottle and you will find a domed shape underneath. This bottom third will be the top of your puppet's head.

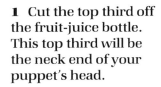

3 Make a few little cuts along the top edge of the bottom third (the edge without the domed shape) so that the two cut sections of the bottle fit easily into each other. Overlap the sections by a couple of centimetres and stick them together with masking tape. You now have a very good basic head shape.

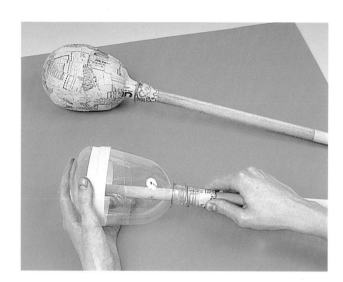

4 Push the rod up into the head. Cover the head and neck joint with three or four layers of newspaper dipped in PVA glue (diluted one part glue to one part water), smoothing down each layer carefully as you put it on.

5 Make a nose by folding a strip of glued newspaper seven or eight times. Cut it to shape and glue it on to the head with more bits of newspaper. Leave to dry. When thoroughly dry, smooth the head down with sandpaper.

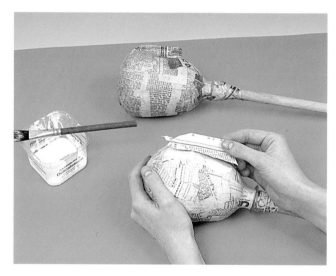

6 Make a simple little calico hand to fit two or three of your fingers. Follow the system you used when making finger puppets (see pages 8–10).

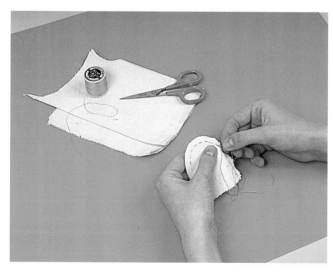

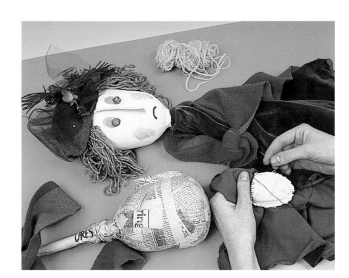

7 Paint and decorate your puppet's head. Make a costume as you did for the paper-bag puppets (see pages 19–22). Sew the hand into position as you did with the glove (see page 17). If the hand needs a touch of colour to match the head, use a little diluted ink or dye.

8 Your puppet is now complete. You will find this a very expressive puppet.

Polystyrene rod puppets

You will need a polystyrene ball, a screwdriver, a dowel rod, PVA glue, a cork, sandpaper, beads, string, scissors, a pencil, a polystyrene ceiling tile, a trimming knife, a piece of wood to use as a cutting block, masking tape, thin white card, two garden rods, a glue brush, powder or tempera paint, a paintbrush, a saucer, calico, and fur fabric, wool or string.

NB Do not use Bostik or UHU, as these glues will dissolve the polystyrene.

1 With the point of the screwdriver, make a hole in the polystyrene ball large enough for the dowel rod to fit into. Glue the rod into position.

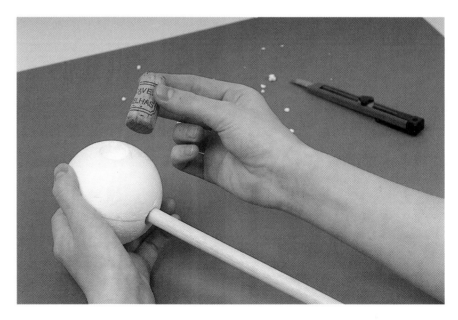

2 Shape one end of the cork with sandpaper, for the puppet's nose. Cut a suitable hole in the polystyrene ball and glue the other end of the cork into position.

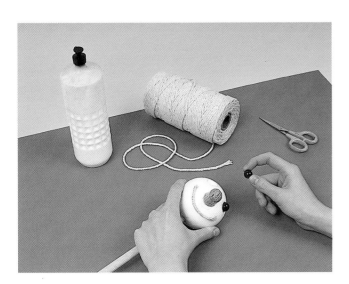

3 Cut shallow holes for the eyes and glue beads in place. Glue on a piece of string to form the mouth.

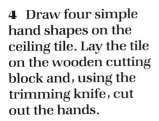

4 Draw four simple hand shapes on the ceiling tile. Lay the tile on the wooden cutting block and, using the trimming knife, cut out the hands.

5 Cut a piece of string, long enough to make both arms when tied round the rod. Tie the middle of the string round the rod and place each end between two hand shapes. Glue each set of two hand shapes together, and hold them in position with masking tape while they are drying.

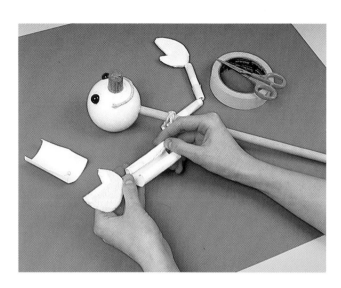

6 Make four arm tubes by rolling pieces of thin white card round the pencil. Thread the card pieces over the string arms and fix them in place with masking tape to form arms which will bend at the elbows and wrists.

7 Shape the hands with the trimming knife and smooth them off with sandpaper. Spike a hole into each hand and glue a garden rod into each. Paint the head and hands with PVA glue to strengthen them then leave them to dry. Make sure your puppet won't stick to anything while drying.

8 When dry, paint the head and hands with tempera or powder paint. Make a costume of painted or plain calico and cut a neck hole. Stick the cloth to the rod neck with masking tape.

9 Decorate your puppet's head with fur fabric, wool or string. Your rod puppet is now complete and ready for action.

To operate the rod puppet, hold the head rod in one hand and the two arm rods in the other. This may feel awkward at first but you will soon get used to it.

Papier mâché glove puppets

You will need a dowel rod, a bottle to use as a modelling stand, clay or plasticine, a spoon for modelling and hollowing the puppet's head, cooking oil, PVA glue, a jar of water, newspaper, sandpaper, a pen, a trimming knife, thin card, a glue brush, masking tape, powder or tempera paint, a paintbrush, a saucer, bits and pieces for decorating your puppet (felt, string, beads, Vilene etc.), a needle and thread, and an old glove.

Cover all working surfaces before you start, as both clay and papier mâché are messy to work with. Wear an apron or old shirt and wash off any spilt glue before it dries.

1 Stand the dowel rod in the bottle and model a head on to it with clay or plasticine. Make the features bold and simple, as fine detail will get lost when you cover the head with paper. When you have finished the modelling, smooth the head with cooking oil to make separation easier when you come to hollow out the clay.

2 Mix up some PVA glue (diluted one part glue to one part water). Dip postage-stamp-size bits of newspaper into the glue mix and place them on to the modelled clay head, overlapping them each time and smoothing down each piece. Five or six layers of newspaper will be needed. When finished, leave the head to dry overnight in a warm place.

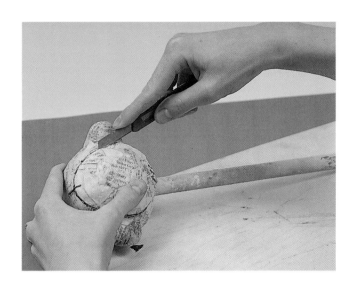

3 When the head is dry, smooth it off with sandpaper. Draw a large circle over the top and back of the head. (Mark a few lines across the circle to help you match up the pieces when you have to rejoin the head.) Now cut out the circle with the trimming knife. If your papier mâché is very thick it can be quite tough, so get some help from a responsible adult.

4 With the spoon, carefully remove all the clay from both halves of the head. If parts of the papier mâché are too thin, paste more paper on to the inside of the head.

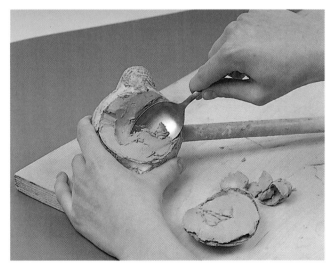

5 Remove the dowel rod. Match up the two halves of the head again and join them with strips of glued paper.

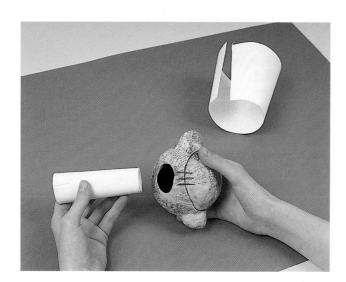

6 Roll some thin card round your index and second finger to make a neck tube. Paint the overlapping card with glue and hold it together with masking tape while drying. Cut a neck hole in the head to fit the neck tube. Fix it in place with more glued newspaper and leave to dry thoroughly.

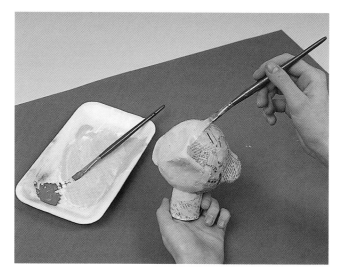

8 Smooth off the neck and head with sandpaper, and paint with powder or tempera paints.

9 Decorate the head with eyes, hair and a hat. This puppet has a cardboard hat covered with felt and his hair is sisal string painted with dye (just lay the string on newspaper and paint it). The eyes are little wooden beads cut in half. The ruff is a long strip of Vilene folded and sewn at one end, top and bottom then tied round the neck.

10 The body is very easy to make. It is simply a glove with a few felt circles sewn on to the front.

Your first two fingers work the head; your thumb becomes one of the puppet's hands and your little finger and the next one become the puppet's second hand. These last two fingers need to move together so that the puppet doesn't appear to have too many arms. If you are making a girl puppet you could sew a skirt on to your glove just below the thumb.

This puppet has a lot of very good movements. By twisting the two neck fingers, you can make him shake his head. He can nod, bow, pick up props, jump up and down when happy, and clap his hands. He can also look very sad.

String scarf puppets

You will need a cardboard box, a pencil, scissors, Bostik, PVA glue, a glue brush, powder or tempera paints, paintbrushes, a saucer, an old scarf (silk or cotton give the best movement), masking tape, black thread (linen carpet thread) or thin string, a large needle, and a coat-hanger.

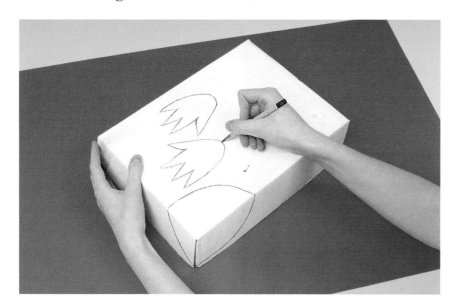

1 Draw the puppet's head on to a corner of the cardboard box. The top of the head should be flat. Draw the hands on to the box as well. Keep the hand shapes simple so that the fingers don't break off.

2 Cut out the face and hands and fold the fingers a little to make a more three-dimensional shape.

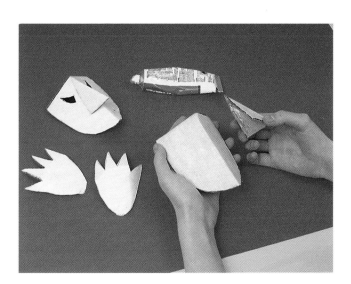

3 Cut out a cardboard nose and stick it on to the face with Bostik. Draw and carefully cut out eyes. To strengthen your puppet, give the face and hands a coat of PVA glue. When the glue is dry, paint the puppet with white or coloured paints.

4 Using masking tape, fix the head and hands to three corners of the scarf, leaving the fourth corner free to trail behind the puppet.

5 Thread the needle with the thread or string and knot the end. Bring the needle up from the palm of one of the puppet's hands and tie the thread or string at one end of the coat hanger. The length of your string should equal the distance from your elbow to 38cm from the ground. Now do the string for the other hand. The two head strings go from the widest points at the top of the head to two points about 13cm apart at the center of the coat hanger.

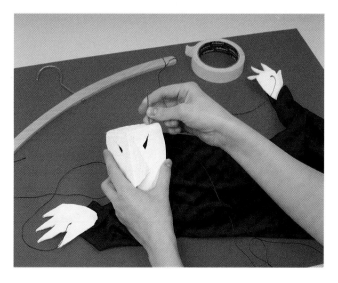

6 Your puppet is now complete and you will find it very exciting to work. You can either just hold the coat-hanger and whoosh the puppet around or you can lift a hand or head string separately. The movements can be quite magical and very ghostly if you do them slowly.

You will need thin white card, a pencil, scissors, a hole punch, Indian inks, dyes or felt pens, cooking oil, brass paper fasteners, masking tape, garden rods, UHU glue, a screen, and a light.

1 Draw the various pieces of your puppet on to the card. Allow for the fact that when you have a joint, the card will need to overlap. Remember that the joints will give you movement, so plan your puppet accordingly.

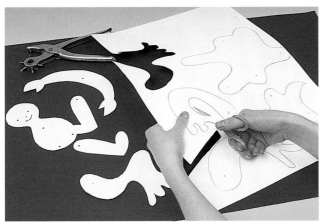

2 Carefully cut out the various pieces and punch holes for the joints.

3 Paint the pieces with Indian inks, dyes or felt pens. Keep the colours strong and paint both sides of each piece – hold them up to a window to make sure both sides match.

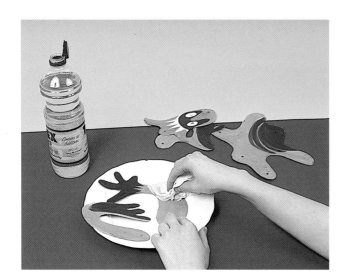

4 When the pieces are dry, rub them thoroughly on both sides with cooking oil. Keep oiling them until they become translucent, then rub off any extra oil.

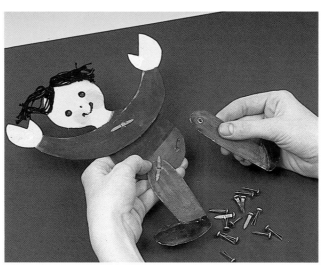

5 Now join the pieces together with the brass paper fasteners. Keep all the smooth heads of the fasteners on one side. This will be the side of the puppet which is held against the screen.

6 Roll a piece of masking tape round one end of each rod. Glue one rod (masking tape end) to each of the puppet's hands. (Use UHU glue, as it will stick to the oiled card.)

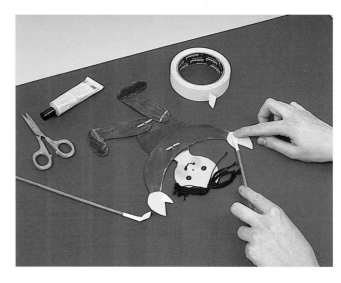

7 The puppeteer's view of the screen.

8 The audience's view.

The screen can be made of stretched calico sheeting, window blind fabric, architect's linen or any material which will let the shadow of the puppet show without the light element being too noticeable – this is very tiring on the audience's eyes.

A 100-watt reading lamp or projection light will be suitable. Keep the light either higher or lower than the puppeteers so that only the puppets show on the screen, not the puppeteers' shadows.

Get some help with the setting up of the light, as it needs to be very stable.

You will need two cardboard boxes of the same size (wine boxes are a good size and are strong), a pencil, scissors, powder or tempera paint, paintbrushes, a jar of water, a saucer, masking tape, garden rods, thin card, thin wire for hooks (paper clips could be bent to shape), a torch, and cellophane or cinemoid.

1 Mark a proscenium or stage opening on to the front of one of the boxes and cut out the opening.

2 Paint the outside of the box, as well as the inside floor and the inside back wall. The inside back wall will be your final backcloth or skycloth.

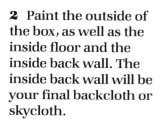

3 Draw and paint the scenery on pieces of card from the second box. This scenery will slide into the first box.

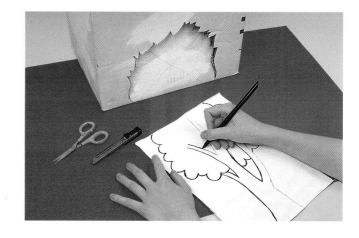

4 Using masking tape, stick a garden rod along the top of each piece of scenery. Allow extra at either end, so that the rods stick out beyond the width of the box.

5 Put the scenery in place by resting the rods in grooves cut in the top of the box sides.

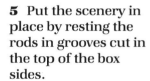

6 Draw and paint puppets on thin card then cut them out. Paint the backs of the puppets on the reverse of the card, so that the puppets can turn round.

7 Using masking tape, fix garden rods to the puppets as you did with the shadow puppets (see pages 37–39). Now fix wire hooks to the rods. Position the hooks so that when the puppets are hooked to the scenery, they will be able to stand without being held. This is especially useful if you are doing a one-man show.

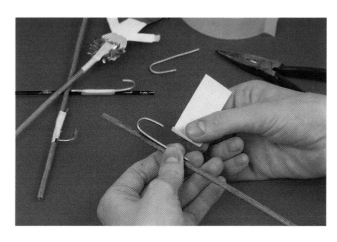

8 Cut lighting slots in one side of the box so that you can use a torch to spotlight the puppets. Make exciting colour changes in your lighting by sticking coloured cellophane or cinemoid over the lighting slots.

9 A finished toy theatre in action.

1 For this stage you need two chairs and three pieces of wood. Tie two upright pieces to the chairs, top and bottom. Now tie the third piece across to form a playboard. Hang a piece of material from the playboard to hide your puppeteers. Scenery can be drawn, cut out and pinned to the upright pieces of wood, thus leaving a good acting area in the centre for your puppets.

This same stage could be used for string puppets. You would then hold the puppets out over the playboard and work them on the floor. A reading lamp or two could be very useful to light the puppets.

2 For this 'Doorway Shadow Theatre', you need to fix an old sheet across a doorway. You may need an adult's help. Choose a doorway that won't be needed while you rehearse and perform. Now fix another, thicker cloth across the bottom of the door, so that the shadow of your head is just out of view when you kneel.

Shine a light on to the sheet. A 100-watt light bulb is usually strong enough for a shadow screen. Mount it higher than your head so that your own shadow isn't thrown on the screen.

Try some special effects with your light. You will find that by moving towards the light, some small sections of your puppets can be blown up to fill the screen without losing any of the detail or blurring their form.

Your audience will sit on the other side of the screen to watch the show.

Stationers and/or artists' materials shops will carry the majority of the items listed in this book. Specialist materials (or materials in large quantities) can be purchased through E J Arnold & Son, Parkside, Leeds LS11 STD9 or Dryad Reeve, Northgate, Leicester.

Adhesives

PVA Evo-stik Wood Adhesive, Extrafast, is excellent for papier mâché, polystyrene, and most surfaces that don't need instant sticking. Any excess will wash off when wet. Bostik Clear will stick most surfaces instantly, but do *not* use it on polystyrene as it will dissolve the surface. UHU is the best glue for oiled shadow figures.

Dyes

Dylon Cold Water Dyes are ideal for painting cloth, but ignore the instructions printed on the container, as these refer to dyeing fabric by soaking it. Instead, mix the dye in a jar with a little cold water, and test the colour first on a small piece of cloth. Remember that the colour will always dry lighter.

Felt pens

Water-based felt pens are best for drawing on cloth puppets, as you can get interesting effects by spreading the colours with a wet brush. But water-based felt pens are not waterproof, so you will have to keep your puppets very clean as they won't stand washing. Spirit-based felt pens are more waterproof and are the best ones to use on plastics, but you can't spread the colours.

Lighting

When lighting your puppets, a couple of reading lamps with 100-watt bulbs will probably be enough. You can use coloured cellophane to change the colour of your lights, but don't put it too near a hot lamp for long as it will burn. An alternative to coloured cellophane is cinemoid, a non-inflammable colour filter for theatre lights. You can buy packs of cinemoid offcuts in mixed colours from: Rand Strand Electrics Ltd, Great West Road, Brentford, Middlesex. If you want to try complicated lighting, Theatre Projects Ltd, 10 Long Acre, London WC2 should be able to help.

Since the beginning of time, people have performed either in praise of their gods or to entertain themselves or members of their tribe. Sometimes they performed as actors and sometimes as puppeteers, giving life or movement to objects such as pieces of wood or clay to tell their story. These objects were carved to represent the figures in the story. In time moving arms and legs were added to make the figures life-like, and so puppets as we know them probably began.

In the tombs of ancient China, India, Egypt and Greece we find remnants of these early puppets. The early Greek figures are very similar to puppets still used in Sicily and Belgium today. An iron rod is fixed to the head, and the arms and legs are worked by strings or rods.

Puppets are easily transported. As the Ancient Greeks moved around, it is likely that they carried puppets on their journeys, thus introducing them to other countries such as Italy. We know that the Romans had both marionettes and glove puppets. And when the Roman Empire finally fell and the places of entertainment closed, the puppeteers packed up and joined the acrobats, jugglers and other minstrels who wandered all over Europe performing in castles and market places.

The early Christian Church found puppets a useful way of telling Bible stories to people who couldn't read or write.

In Italy, in the 15th century, puppets were involved in the *Commedia dell'Arte*, a set of stories about a group of masked clowns, some of whom we still know today as Harlequin, Scaramuch and Punch. These clowns each had very distinctive characteristics and would work to a prearranged plot but with improvised dialogue, much as our Punch and Judy performers do today. The *Commedia dell'Arte* shows were such a success in Italy that the puppeteers and actors took them to the rest of Europe, where they were met with great enthusiasm.

But puppetry has had its ups and downs through the centuries. During the Elizabethan Age, an Act was passed by Parliament which made strolling players and puppeteers criminals unless they were granted a royal licence by a rich patron. These restrictions made it difficult for the players and puppeteers to continue with their careers.

In 1642 Oliver Cromwell banned live theatre but not puppet theatre; so the puppets played to full houses. For many years the puppets alone kept the English theatre alive.

When Charles II returned to England in 1660 to take up the throne once more, he was followed by entertainers and puppeteers who came to help the people celebrate.

In the 18th century puppets became fashionable among Society's lords and ladies. There were many thriving theatres in the West End of London and in Bath. But by the end of the century the well-to-do had tired of their new-found toy, so the puppets were thrown back into the fairs and the streets.

Street performances became very popular. The 'Punchmen' or puppeteers spent most of the year in London or one of the other big cities, but when summer came they would head for the coast and perform on the beaches to the new middle-classes who were now beginning to take holidays.

The fairground marionette companies continued to tour, carrying, in horse-drawn carts, entire wooden theatres to seat a few hundred people which they would assemble at fairs or on village greens around the country. These theatres were worked by families who jealously guarded their skills and tricks. No one outside the family was allowed to see how the puppets were worked.

With the coming of the First World War, the puppets were packed up and stored in warehouses and barns around the country. Most were forgotten, but now there is a great revival of interest in the puppet theatre. Many very good companies using string, rod, glove and shadow puppets tour the country. Some have settled down in permanent homes in theatres in London, Norwich and Birmingham.

Keep a look-out for them, and when you see a show or put one on yourself remember that you are involved in one of the oldest forms of theatre in the world.

Museum collections and Puppet theatres

These are some of the places you can visit or contact to find out more about puppets. For more information specific to your area contact The Puppet Centre Trust, Battersea Arts Centre, Lavender Hill, London SW11 5TN Tel: 020 7228 5335.

Museum of Childhood
Cambridge Heath Road
London E2 9PA
www.museumofchildhood.org.uk
A good general collection

The Horniman Museum
100 London Road
Forest Hill
London SE23 3PQ
www.horniman.ac.uk
Puppets and masks from all over the world

The Theatre Museum
1e Tavistock Street
Covent Garden
London WC2E 7PR
www.theatremuseum.vam.ac.uk
Houses the British Puppet and Model Theatre Guild's collection

The Museum of Childhood
34 High Street
Royal Mile
Edinburgh
www.cac.org.uk

Liverpool Museum
William Brown Street
Liverpool L3 8EN
www.liverpoolmuseums.org.uk
Collection of Javanese shadow puppets

Pitt Rivers Museum
South Parks Road
Oxford OX1 3PP
www.prm.ox.ac.uk
Collection of shadow figures

Hove Museum and Art Gallery
19 New Church Road
Hove
BN3 4AB
www.hove.virtualmuseum.info

Performing Arts Collection of South Australia
Adelaide Festival Centre
King William Street
Adelaide SA
www.pacsa.asn.au

Puppet Theatres
The theatres listed all have regular performances of puppet plays. Some of them tour and also offer workshops and other educational activities.

Little Angel Theatre
14 Dagmar Passage
London N1 2DN
020 7226 1787
www.littleangeltheatre.com

Norwich Puppet Theatre
St James
Whitefriars
Norwich NR3 1TN
01603 615564
www.puppettheatre.co.uk

Polka Children's Theatre
240 The Broadway
Wimbledon
London SW19 1SB
020 8543 4888
www.polkatheatre.com

Purves Puppets and Biggar Puppet Theatre
Puppet Tree House
Broughton Road
Biggar
Lanakshire
MI12 6HA
01899 220631
www.purvespuppets.com

Harlequin Puppet Theatre
Rhos on Sea
Colwyn Bay
Wales
01492 548166
www.puppets.inuk.com

The Puppet Barge
A travelling, floating theatre.
www.puppetbarge.com
020 7249 6876

Spare Parts Puppet Theatre
PO Box 897
Fremantle
WA 6959
Australia
08 9335 5044
www.sppt.asn.au/famehome.htm